Russian Swear Words

A Systematic Guide to Fluent Russian Swearing

By Vovan Otradniy

Table of Contents

-1-

Introduction

Why most Russian swearing books don't work and this one does.

Open up your average slang dictionary. It doesn't matter if it's French, American or Russian. What is the main problem there? Well, if you buy most American slang book targeted at Russians you will notice that they seem to be quite extensive. However, usually 80% of the terms included in those slang books are, well, worthless, for lack of a better word.

Phrases that hadn't been used since the 60s, weird 80s slang or expressions used in some lone obscure of the country. How often do you say "I porked out at that restaurant last night"? Or how many times have you used the term "hot rod" in the last 12 months? If your age is below 65, my guess is the count on those instances is pretty close to zero.

And imagine how weird a foreign speaker would sound when trying to use all these out of date, regional and other obscure slang expressions when speaking English? It will be funny but not in a way the speaker intends perhaps. So that's something to think about.

Then why all these useless words are in those dictionaries? I don't know but I think there's absolutely no good reason why they should be there. Many or most slang words in all languages come and go but the few remain.

In English some words date to the 80s or the 60s and sound funny today, but others like "fuck" or "bitch" have been around forever and will probably stay that way.

So, what does all of this have to do with swearing in Russian? Dissatisfied with availability of quality material and systems that teach how to swear in Russian, I decided to develop my own.

First of all, this book will not contain a lot of everyday slang. It is focused solely on swearing and dirty Russian in particular. Unlike others, it doesn't stuff the pages with millions of swear words and expressions that are outdated, uncommon or simply not used enough to justify inclusion.

Instead, we will focus on the fundamentals, those words that every Russian who swears will use. We will learn how Russian swearing differs from American swearing, how every word must be used to be used effectively and steps you can take to swear not like a funny American who got a book with a bunch of slang no one uses, but swear like other Russians do.

We will not try to make up for lack of organization or systematic thought with humor. Instead, we will use an organized, precise system that will enable you to swear using words that are actually used. For every mentioned examples be sure to construct three of your own; this should be plenty of practice

-2-

Fundamentals of Swearing

In Russian

The main words you need to know to swear effectively in Russian.

Russian swearing is not terribly different from American swearing as far as the intent of it goes. So, what are the reasons you may want to learn swearing in Russian, just like in English?

First of all, swearing is used for emphasis. For example, the phrase "What the fuck was that?" is not different from meaning of "What was that?" The main difference is the emphasis that makes the phrase stronger, more poignant and expresses your strong or aggressive feelings about the issue in a more powerful way.

Secondly, swearing is used for personal attacks. For example: "You dirty fucking bastard" is much more powerful than "You not very good person". People frown down on swearing but it really does express a form and feeling, which cannot be expressed in any other way. Thus, in this way swearing can be very apt and powerful.

Lastly, swearing is often used for talking dirty or to enhance our sexual experiences.

Russian swearing is not different in this regard. In this chapter we will introduce the basis of Russian swearing that will then be applied to two main areas: Emphasis and Personal Attacks. The coming chapters will explore some other relevant words

So, without further ado, here are the basic swear words that Russians use on an everyday basis. Note that these are literal meanings. When used for emphasis they don't literally mean what is mentioned below, but just add emphasis to the expression.

Primary Swear Words

Ебать – To fuck.

Блядь – Whore.

Сука - Bitch

Пизда - Cunt

Хуй - Dick

Пидараз/Пидар - Faggot

To fuck is pretty self explanatory and the feel of it is identical to "fuck" in English. The word блядь, on the other hand, is much worse than "whore" in English, which properly wouldn't even be considered a swear word and is more borderline. There are other less offensive ways to say whore or slut in Russian, but блядь is very offensive and very much a swear word. Many English speakers have trouble believing that the word that means whore would be so offensive.

But it really is. On the other hand, notice that the word "shit" is not mentioned above. "Shit" in Russian is a little less offensive than the words above, thus I've included them in the honorable mentions category below.

Honorable Mentions

Говно/дерьмо - Shit

Срать – To Shit

Ссать – To Piss

Гондон – Condom

Shit is not as offensive as some of the words in the Primary category and говно is more offensive than дерьмо. The rest are mildly offensive. Interestingly, the word гондон or condom is an insult in Russian. Most English speakers are pretty amused that you can insult someone by calling them a condom, something you can't do in English. There is another word, презерватив, which usually is not used for insults but гондон is used almost exclusively for that.

Grammar

Ебать or to fuck is conjugated in the following way.

Imperfective form: Ебать

(Present tense)

Я ебу

Ты ебешь

Он/Она ебет

Мы ебем

Вы ебете

Они ебут

Imperfective Past Tense:

Он ебал

Она ебала

Вы/Они ебали

Perfective form: Поебать, Выебать, Отъебать.

The perfective has several different forms different in emphasis but all emphasizing the same thing. The rest are conjugated the same way, just change the prefix.

Я поебу

Ты поебешь

Он/Она поебет

Мы поебем

Вы поебете

Они поебут

Thus, this is how the verb ебать is conjugated. The rest of the nouns are declined according to standard declension rules so those are self explanatory.

-3-

Swearing for Emphasis

Put more punch into your Russian phrases.

The following is a list of words that are used for emphasis solely to show strong feelings, anger, disgust, amusement, surprise or just about any other strong emotion. Now let's do a series of case studies to get a feel of how these work.

Ебать – To fuck.

Here is how this word is used for emphasis in Russian:

1. Ебанный – Fucking. This converts fuck into an adjective. Then, same as in English, you can attach this adjective to just about anything to demonstrate your strong feelings about it. Note that ебанный as an adjective is most often used about inanimate things, usually when something is not up to your standard. So, this part is the same as English. But in English, you can say, for example, "I fucking told you to do it". Can't use it like that. Also, when you say ебанный about something in Russian it's always negative. So you can't say "That's fucking awesome" in Russian, as calling something ебанный always gives it a negative connotation. So keep that in mind. Here are some typical examples of how it's used.

Example 1: Ебанный компьютер не работает!

Translation: The fucking computer doesn't work.

Example 2: Ебанная школа закрыта сегодня из за снега.

Translation: The fucking school is closed today because of the snow.

Example 3: Мой ебанный профессор поставил мне два.

Translation: My fucking professor gave me an F.

2. Ебать. Just like in English, sometimes you can just say ебать for emphasis. That can be used to indicate just about any emotion. It can be positive or negative. Usually though, it includes elements of amazement and surprise.

Example 1: Ебать! Сколько здесь пива!?

Translation: Fuck, there's a lot of beer here. (not a literal translation) Demonstrates amazement/surprise.

Example 2: Ебать! Какая девушка! Demonstrates amazement.

Translation: Fuck! What a girl!

Example: Ебать! Сигареты кончились! Demonstrates disappointment.

Translation: Fuck! I ran out of cigarettes

Блядь – Whore.

Блядь is the quintessential Russian swearword. For the words used purely for emphasis, with no additional meaning, блядь is usually the most common words that everyone from construction workers to oligarchs mince their phrases with. A very common short version of блядь is бля.

Блядь or бля is extremely adaptable and can be used just about in any sentence. It can demonstrate just about anything, from anger to surprise. And you're not calling anyone a whore, just adding emphasis. In this way it is similar to ебать. However, бля is often used by people just in everyday speech without something extraordinarily surprising taking place (which is the case with ебать).

Here are its most common emphatic uses.

1. Surprise or disappointment. Usually, блядь goes either in the very beginning or at the very end of the sentence

Example 1: Блядь! Что случилось?

Translation: Shit! What happened? (Literally it's "Whore! What happened?" but I am changing it to "shit" so it makes more sense in English)

Example 2: Магазин закрылся? Блядь!

Translation: Store is closed? Shit!

2. Anger. Often during a confrontation блядь is used to taunt the offender.

Example 1: Ты что здесь сделал, бля?

Translation: What the fuck did you do here?

Example 2: Ты что, блядь, думаешь тебе все можно?

Translation: You fucking think you can do whatever you want?

3. Any other reason whatsoever. Many people enjoy using word not just occasionally but in every sentence, regardless of the situation (taxi drivers, construction workers and teenagers are such groups). To use this word, you can stick it in the beginning of a sentence, at the very end and very often in the middle somewhere. It's hard to go wrong with блядь, stick it pretty much anywhere and it's gonna work.

Example 1: Я блядь пошел на концерт.

Translation: I fucking went to that concert.

Example 2: Да там блядь много людей блядь.

Translation: Fucking too many fucking people over there.

Example 3: Я эту блядь книгу читал блядь два часа так блядь и ничего не понял.... блядь!

Translation: I read this fucking book for fucking two hours and never fucking learned anything… fuck!

Starting to sound like a script for Big Lebowski, right? Now you'd say surely nobody talks like this… all I gotta say is you'd be surprised. It's certainly not common to blend that many блядь's in a sentence but it's not unheard of. And people in the US talk like that too.

I wouldn't recommend to use блядь as often as in the last example, but once or twice per sentence is standard and more often is not unheard of. If you want to master it, listen to when an how other Russians use it and imitate them.

Сука - Bitch

This word is unique in that it is traditionally a swear word but the elitists also admit it as a literary word that is ok to use under certain contexts in polite circles. However, we won't learn it in that context. As far as usage goes, сука is identical to блядь. Stick it at the end, beginning or middle of just about any sentence and it adds emphasis.

1. Surprise or disappointment. Usually, блядь goes either in the very beginning or at the very end of the sentence

Example 1: Сука! Где они?

Translation: Shit! Where are they?

Example 2: Кинотеатр закрылся? Сука!

Translation: Store is closed? Shit!

2. Anger. Often during a confrontation сука is used to taunt the offender.

Example 1: Где мои деньги, сука?

Translation: Where's my money, bitch?

Example 2: Ты что, сука, так разговариваешь с моей девушкой?

Translation: Why are you talking to my girl like that, bitch?

3. Any other reason whatsoever. Same as with блядь, use it at any part of the sentence.

Example 1: Я сука пошел в ресторан.

Translation: I fucking went to that restaurant.

The rest of examples are the same as with блядь. So, to make it more fun let's see how we can blend the two. Doing this is very common. Just put блядь in front of in front of сука or the other way around and you've doubled the emphasis effect. Easy!

Example 2: Этот сука блядь магазин закрыт опять.

Translation: This motherfucking store is closed again.

Example 3: Этот блядь водитель сука нас везет не туда…. блядь!

Translation: This motherfucking driver fucking doesn't know where he's going… fuck!

That's right, you can stick these just about anywhere you want. But listen to how other Russians use it to get it perfect. As you can see, the combinations of where you can put them are endless.

Пизда – Cunt.

While the word пизда itself is not used for emphasis, a close derivative of it is used very often in the Russian language. That word is пиздец. It has no objective meaning, other than the emphasis. If you say пиздец, it doesn't mean cunt nor is it used to denote any concrete object. Normally, it is just used to emphasize something extraordinary, whether good or bad. An explosion, an unexpected drop in the course of a rouble, winning the lottery, your girlfriend cheating on you, finding a suitcase stuffed with money, the craziness of all these situations can be summarized in just one word: пиздец.

Note that пиздец cannot be used to insult someone or just as random emphasis everywhere. This word is reserved for truly extraordinary situations and thus you normally wouldn't use it quite as often in a sentence as блядь or сука. There is no good way to translate it into English, but I usually use "Holy shit!" or "Fucking a". Note that these don't capture the full meaning of it but are as close as it gets.

Example 1: Сегодня курс рубля упал на 10%. Пиздец!

Translation: Today the rouble fell by 10%. Fucking a!

Example 2: Мне сегодня заплатили $10 000. Пиздец!

Translation: I got paid $10 000 today. Fucking a!

Example 3: Я мою девушку поймал с другим парнем. Пиздец!

Translations: I caught my girl with another guy. Fucking a!

Believe it or not, that's it. These are the main phrases used to express emphasis in Russian. Now Russian is unique in that you can combine and recompile all of these phrases, adding all those little endings to change the emphasis a bit. Also, there are quite a few variations drawn off these words. For example, бляха муха is often used interchangeably with пиздец. However, it is obvious that this is a variation on блядь. Бляха is formed from блядь and муха just means fly. So, literally it means something like fucked up fly but is used interchangeably with пиздец. There are many of these variations but most of time people will just say блядь, ебать, сука or пиздец, so we'll just focus on those. Besides, the rest of these expressions often come in and out of style, rendering them useless. But as far as Russian swearing form emphasis goes, блядь, ебать, сука and пиздец form the core of all Russian swearing. They were used by poets from Esenin to Pushkin hundreds of years ago and are still used by everyone today. The chances that they will disappear or go out of style in the near future are slim to none.

Honorable mentions

Ебанный в рот – Fucked in the mouth. Usually used interchangeably with пиздец.

Еб твою мать – Fuck your mother. Used interchangeably with пиздец.

На хуй – To a dick. Used interchangeably with блядь.

-4-

Blending Swearwords for Emphasis

Blend them to magnify the effect.

We've done this a bit before but let's practice this more so you can gain a better understanding of exactly how this works.

Again, the three main words we have is: ебанный, сука, блядь and пиздец.

Let's take any regular sentence and practice infusing it with emphasis through all these great swear words we've learned.

Example 1: Ты что не видел этот фильм?

Translation: What, you haven't seen this movie?

Example 1 + Swearing: Ты что, бля, не видел этот фильм?

Translation: What, you haven't seen this fucking film?

Example 2: Все, я пошел за пивом.

Translation: That's it, I'm going to get some beer,

Example 2 + Swearing: Все, бля, я пошел за пивом, сука.

Translation: That's fucking it, I'm going to get some beer, bitch.

Example 3: Где моя шапка?

Translation: Where's my hat?

Example 3 + Swearing: Сука, где моя шапка, блядь? Пиздец!

Translation: Bitch, where's my fucking hat? Fuck!

Example 4: Спартак вчера опять проиграл.

Translation: Spartak lost again yesterday.

Example 4 + Swearing: Ебанный Спартак, сука, вчера опять, блядь, проиграл. Сука ебанная!

Translation: Fucking Spartak, bitch, yesterday fucking lost the fucking game again. Motherfucking bitch!

Example 5: Что это за суп? Да еще так дорого?

Translation: What kind of soup is this? And at such a price?

Example 5 + Swearing: Блядь, что это за суп сука? Да еще сука так дорого? Пиздец блядь!

Translation: Fuck, what kind of soup is this, bitch? And at so fucking expensive? Fuck me (Or Fucking a)!

Example 6: Где мои часы?

Translation: Where's my watch?

Example 6 + Swearing: Где эти ебанные часы, сука блядь?

Translation: Where is this fucking watch, motherfucker?

Let's try rearranging the above sentences using the honorable mentions: ебанный в рот, еб твою мать and на хуй.

Example 7: Опять кошелек дома забыл?

Translation: Left the wallet at home again?

Example 7 + Swearing: Опять кошелек дома забыл блядь? Ебать!

Translation: You left the fucking wallet at home again? Fuck!

Example 1: Что это за суп? Да еще так дорого?

Translation: What kind of soup is this? And at such a price?

Example 1 + Swearing: Блядь, что это за суп, ебанный в рот? Да еще так дорого на хуй? Еб твою мать, блядь!

Translation: Fuck, what kind of soup is this, motherfucker? And at so fucking expensive? Fuck me (Or Fucking a)!

Example 2: Где мои часы?

Translation: Where's my watch?

Example 2 + Swearing: Где эти часы, на хуй? Ебаный в рот!

Translation: Where the fuck is this watch? Fuck!

Example 3: Спартак вчера опять проиграл.

Translation: Spartak yesterday lost again.

Example 3 + Swearing: Спартак, сука, вчера опять, на хуй, проиграл. Еб твою мать, сука!
Translation: Fucking Spartak yesterday again fucking lost, bitch. Fucking a, motherfucker!

As you can see, many of these words can be used interchangeable and placed in the beginning or at the end of any sentence to add emphasis.

-5-

Personal Attacks

Tell them all you think about them.

Personal attacks are the other main reason most people use swear words in any language and Russian is no different. Thus, let's outline the main words that can be used to insult someone.

Блядь - Slut. This one is a universal insult and can be used on anyone, male or female.

Derivatives (these mean basically the same thing with varying emphasis): Бля, проблядушка, блядина, блядища.

Verb: Блядовать – To Whore Around.

Adjective. Блядский - Whoreish

Noun. Блядство - Slutiness

Example 1: Твоя девушка блядь!

Translation: Your girlfriend is a slut!

Example 2:: Ты на блядь старую похож с Тверской!

Translation: You look like an old slut from Tverskaya!

Говно – Shit. Unlike English, the word is not used for emphasis. It is also rarely used as an insult. However, numerous words that are derived from говно are very common insults.

Example 1: Говно твой Спартак!

Translation: Your Spartak is shit!

Example 2: Что это за говно?

Translation: What kind of shit is this?

Говнюк – Shithead. This insult is quite common. Usually refers to a backstabber or someone of questionable moral integrity.

Example 1: Твой друг Дима говнюк.

Translation: Your friend Dima is a shithead.

Example 2: Это что за говнюк?

Translation: What shithead is this?

Говноед – Shiteater. Not as common as it once was, this word is still used enough to merit mention. Can be used on anyone you don't like.

Example 1: Ты говноед!

Translation: You're a shiteater!

Говно на палочке – Shit on a stick. An expression that is getting a little dated (but still used), use this one if you want something more creative.

Example 1: Это не команда, это говно на палочке!

Translation: That's not a team, that's shit on a stick!

Гондон – Condom (Douchebag). Russian is unique in that you can insult someone by calling them a condom. Similar to говнюк, this usually refers to a backstabber or someone of questionable moral qualities and intentions. Thus, this insult puts down NOT the person's intelligence, but their moral character. Douchebag might be the closest American analogue. This one doesn't have derivatives but is one of the most popular insults in its own right.

Example 1: Ты что сделал, гондон?

Translation: What did you do, douchebag (condom)?

Example 2: Почему? Потому что он гондон!

Translation: Why? Because he's a douchebag (condom).

Ебанный – Fucking. Same as emphasis, just add this to any other insult to amplify the moral damage. Has the largest number of offshoots that are even more common. These follow below.

Example 1: Надоела мне твоя ебанная музыка.

Translation: I'm sick of your fucking music.

Example 2: Ебанный компьютер сломался!

Translation: Fucking computer broke down!

Долбоеб – Dumbfuck. Derived from ебать, this is one of the most common insults in the Russian language. It is always used to put down someone's intellectual abilities or poor decision making, not their moral character or intent so keep that in mind.

Example 1: Он что долбоеб!?

Translation: Is he a dumbfuck?

Example 2: Иди отсюда, долбоеб!

Translation: Get out of here, you dumbfuck!

Ебало – Ugly mug. A swear word that refers to someone's face, this one's often used and often leads to violence.

Example 1: Ебало заткни!

Translation: Shut your ugly mug!

Ебальник – Same as Ебало.

Ебанат – Same as долбоеб.

Example 1: Твой друг ебанат!

Translation: Your friend is a dumbfuck!

Ебанутый – Fucked in the head. Rearrange ебанный a bit and you have fucked in the head. This is a full analogue to the American expression so use it as such.

Example 1: Ебанутый он какой то!

Translation: He's kind of fucked in the head!

Ебанушка – Fuck up. Someone extremely irrational, stupid or awkward.

Example 1: Пошел отсюда, ебанушка!

Translation: Get out of here, you fuck up!

Отъебись – Fuck off. Perfect equivalent to the English counterpart.

Example 1: Хватит мне звонить. Отъебись!

Translation: Enough calling me. Fuck off!

Example 2: Отъебись от меня!

Translation: Fuck off!

Уебок – Same as ебанушка.

Example 1: Дима уебок!

Translation: Dima is a fuck up!

Уебан – Same as ебанушка.

Example 1: Твой друг уебан!

Translation: Your friend is a fuck up!

Жопа – An ass. This is a very mild insult compared to others in here but its frequency of use justifies its inclusion. Meaning is same as its American analogue.

Example 1: Вот ты жопа!

Translation: You're quite an ass!

Жопа с ушами –Ass with ears. Same as previous.

Example 1: Ты жопа с ушами!

Translation: You're an ass with ears!

Жопа с ручкой – Ass with a handle. Same as previous two but with more creativity.

Example 1: Она жопа с ручкой.

Translation: She's an ass with a handle!

Жополиз – Asslicker. Just means a bootlicker, someone that kisses someone else's ass too much.

Example 1: Я давно знаю, что он жополиз.

Translation: I've know for some time he's an asslicker.

Мудак – Moron. Moron is the closes word but мудак is a bit more offensive. Regardless, it refers to someone stupid or irrational.

Example 1: Вот ты мудак!

Translation: You're a moron!

Мудило – Variation on мудак.

Example 1: Ты не знал что он мудило?

Translation: You didn't know he's a moron?

Мудозвон – Another variation that means the same thing.

Example 1: Потому что ты мудозвон!

Translation: Because you're a moron!

Пидараз – Faggot. Faggot is the literal meaning of the word. However, the word is most often used just as a generic insult, with that person not necessarily having anything to do with being gay or even acting metrosexual. So, in practice it often is used interchangeably with "asshole", even though пидараз is a lot more offensive.

Example 1: Зачем ты ей сказал? Пидараз!

Translation: Why did you tell her? Asshole (faggot)!

Педераст – A variation on the original word.

Example 1: Ты педераст!

Translation: You're an asshole! (faggot)

Пидар – Same as above.

Example 1: Где мои деньги, пидар?

Translation: Where's my money, asshole (faggot)?

Педрило – Same as above.

Example 1: Что молчишь, педрило?

Translation: Why are you silent, asshole (faggot)?

Пизда – Cunt. A lot of people get confused with this one and think the word is interchangeable with the word "pussy". It is NOT. Pussy is киска, and пизда means cunt. Most often this word is used as an insult and has a built in negative connotation for many people. Thus, I'd be very careful in using that word to refer to any woman's vagina. However, if you're looking for an insult it is the correct word to use. This is always used about a woman so keep that in mind. And, I'm teaching you this but you better use it responsibly. Be nice to those Russian girls now. But for the sake of education I did put it in.

Example 1: Где эта пизда?

Translation: Where's this cunt?

Манда – Same as пизда but slightly less offensive.

Example 1: Вот манда!

Translation: What a cunt!

Пизданутый – Fucked in the head. Can be used about either male/female.

Example 1: Он пизданутый немного.

Translation: He's a little fucked in the head.

Пизда Ивановна – A humorous variation on the original word. This one is reserved for females.

Пиздюк – A bitter fuck. Usually used about someone with questionable morals and intentions. Used for males usually.

Example 1: Где этот пиздюк?

Translation: Where is this bitter fuck?

Сосать – To Suck. This word is unique in that it can be used as an insult on it's own, without attaching it to any noun or even sentence. If you want to insult someone just yell out СОСАТЬ and that should get your job done (and get you a beating if you're unlucky). Can be used about males or females.

Сука – Bitch. Self explanatory. Can be used for both males and females, same as in English.

Example 1: Ах ты сука!

Translation: You bitch!

Сукин сын – Son of a bitch. Same as English.

Ссученок – Same as сукин сын.

Хуй – Dick. This word is unique in that you can use it both literally as an insult and figuratively to say "fuck you". You can use хуй to call someone a dick but keep in mind, хуй is a lot more offensive than dick. Хуй probably is the most offensive and the most notorious word in the Russian language also known as the three letter word or слово из трех букв.

Иди на хуй – Fuck you (literally go on a dick). Probably the most common Russian insult, this is the equivalent to the English "fuck you".

Example 1: Что ты сказал? Иди на хуй!

Translation: What did you say? Fuck you!

Хуй тебе в рот – Dick in your mouth. Usually used to rebuff somebody when they are asking you for an unreasonable favor.

Example 1: Когда я деньги тебе верну? Хуй тебе в рот, вот когда!

Translation: When will I return your money? Dick in your mouth, that's when!

Хуесос – Cocksucker. Pretty self explanatory.

Example 1: Молчи, хуесос!

Translation: Be quiet, cocksucker!

Хуеплет – Dickbender. Like xyecoc but more creative.

Example 1: Ты хуеплет!

Translation: You're a dickbender!

-6-

Swearing for Everyday Things

When a regular word just doesn't cut it.

Swearing is not used just for emphasis or insults. Sometimes swear words happen to express the meaning of everyday things and are used as such.

This doesn't mean they don't add emphasis or are free from offensive meaning. Actually, they are quite full of both of these things. Regardless, these words are out there and if you want to be an advanced Russian speaker and don't want to be left out of any conversations there will be invaluable.

Бздеть / Набздеть – To Fart.

Example 1: Кто опять набздел?

Translation: Who farted again?

Example 2: Хватит бздеть, сука!

Translation: Stop farting, bitch!

Говниться / Заговниться – To act difficult.

Example 1: Хватит говниться уже!

Translation: Stop acting difficult!

Example 2: Я не понял, что ты говнишься?

Translation: I don't get it, why are you being difficult?

До пизды – Don't give a fuck. (Use with Dative)

Example 1: Мне все до пизды.

Translation: I don't give a fuck about anything.

Example 2: Мне до пизды твой футбольный чемпионат.

Translation: I don't give a fuck about your soccer tournament.

До хуя – A shitload.

Example 1: Там телок до хуя.

Translation: Shitload of chicks there.

Example 2: Смотри, до хуя пива!

Translation: Look, a shitload of beer!

Доебываться / Доебаться – Fuck with.

Example 1: Что ты доебался ко мне, я не понял?

Translation: I don't get it, why are you fucking with me?

Example 2: Слушай, хватит к ней доебываться!

Translation: Listen, stop fucking with her!

Дрочить / Подрочить – Jerk off.

Example 1: Сейчас, подрочу и приду

Translation: Give me a second, let me jerk off and I'll come over.

Example 2: Да ничего он не делает, дома дрочит!

Translation: He isn't doing anything, he's jerking off at home!

Ебать мозги – Fuck with my head (fuck with my brain literally). Means being difficult or unreasonable.

Example 1: Хватит мне ебать мозги уже.

Translation: Enough fucking with my head already.

Example 2: Что ты мозги ебешь здесь, я не понял?

Translation: I don't get it, why are you fucking with my head?

Ебать Му Му – Same as ебать мозги.

Example 1: Ты давай не еби му му здесь.

Translation: Don't fuck with my head now.

Заебись – Fuck yeah.

Example 1: Сигареты есть? Заебись!

Translation: You got smokes? Fuck yeah!

Example 2: Заебись! Сегодня уроки отменили!

Translation: Fuck yeah! Classes got cancelled today!

Заебывать / Заебать – To get sick of.

Example 1: Меня эта училка заебала уже.

Translation: I am fucking sick of this teacher.

Example 2: Как меня заебала эта песня.

Translation: How fucking I am of this song.

Зажопивать / Зажопить – Withhold something valuable.

Example 1: Ты что сигареты зажопил?

Translation: Why did you hide the cigarettes?

Example 2: Хватит жопить пиво от нас!

Translation: Enough hiding beer from us!

Какого хуя? – What the fuck?

Example 1: Какого хуя ты мне не позвонила?

Translation: Why the fuck didn't you call me?

Example 2: Какого хуя он здесь делает?

Translation: What the fuck is he doing here?

Мне по хуй – I don't give a fuck.

Example 1: Поздно? А мне по хуй!

Translation: It's late? I don't give a fuck!

Example 2: Не любишь меня? Мне по хуй!

Translation: You don't love me? I don't give a fuck!

На хуй так делать? – Why the fuck do that?

Example 1: На хуй ты звонишь так поздно?

Translation: Why the fuck are calling so late?

Example 2: На хуй ты ушла так рано?

Translation: Why the fuck did you leave so early?

Наебывать / Наебать – To swindle/cheat someone out of something.

Example 1: Я его наебал на сто баксов.

Translation: I swindled him out of a hundred bucks.

Example 2: Он меня наебал.

Translation: He fucked me over.

Пиздеж – Lies

Example 1: Все это пиздеж.

Translation: All that is lies.

Example 2: Пиздеж этот я устал уже слушать.

Translation: Sick of listening to these lies.

Пиздить / Напиздить – To lie.

Example 1: Что ты пиздишь!?

Translation: Why the fuck are you lying?

Example 2: Не пизди мне.

Translation: Don't fucking lie to me

Пиздить / Спиздить – To steal

Example 1: Кто спиздил зажигалку?

Translation: Who stole the lighter?

Example 2: Он в магазине спиздил бутылку водки.

Translation: He stole a bottle vodka from the store.

Подъебывать / Подъебать – To make fun of.

Example 1: Хватит меня подъебывать.

Translation: Stop making fun of me.

Трахать \ Трахнуть – To fuck. A milder version of fuck, this one is much less offensive.

Example 1: По моему он хочет ее трахнуть.

Translation: I think he wants to fuck her.

Example 2: Давай трахаться!

Translation: Let's fuck.

Хуйня – Nonsense or sucks.

Example 1: Все это хуйня!

Translation: All that is nonsense!

Example 2: Хуйня эта программа!

Translation: This show sucks!

Хуй знает – Fuck knows.

Example 1: Где он? А хуй знает!

Translation: Where is he? Ah, fuck knows!

Example 2: Хуй знает где моя машина сейчас!

Translation: Fuck knows where my car is now!

Хули – Why the fuck?

Example 1: Хули ты так нагло со мной разговариваешь?

Translation: Why the fuck are you talking to me rudely like that?

Example 2: Хули ты орешь?

Translation: Why the fuck are you yelling?

Хуяк – Simulation of a hit or punch (bam).

Example 1: Я хуяк ему в глаз ударил.

Translation: I *bam* hit him in the eye.

Хуярить / Захуярить – To energetically do something or to hit someone.

Example 1: Мы вчера его отхуярили.

Translation: We beat the shit out of him yesterday.

Example 2: Я хуярил на даче огород.

Translation: I was fucking messing with the garden at my dacha.

Хуячить / Нахуячить – Same as хуярить.

Example 1: Я хуячу на метро туда.

Translation: I went there by metro.

Example 2: Классно он его отхуячил.

Translation: The way he fucked him up was awesome

Что за на хуй? - What the fuck?

Example 1: Это что за на хуй?

Translation: What the fuck is this?

-7-

Euphemisms

When you want to soften the effect.

Russian, just like English, has quite a series of euphemisms, which are usually phrases that sound close to their swearword counterparts, but yet without the extreme offensive meaning. The phrases and words below are derived from their offensive counter parts but can be used with less caution.

Твою мать – Euphemism for “fuck your mother” (еб твою мать).

Example 1: Ты что делаешь, твою мать!

Translation: What the fuck are you doing?

На фиг - Euphemism for «на хуй». Normally used for emphasis.

Example 1: Да там на фиг много было людей.

Translation: There were a lot of fucking people there.

Иди на фиг – A milder version of fuck you (иди на хуй), something like “go to hell”.

Example 1: Что ты сказал? Иди ты на фиг!

Translation: What did you say? Screw you!

Фигово – Badly (Euphemism for хуево)

Example 1: Фигово домашнее задание я сделал

Translation: I did a shitty job on this homework.

Хер – Euphemism for dick (хуй).

Example 1: Хер старый этот придет сегодня.

Translation: This old dick will come over today.

На хер - Euphemism for «на хуй». Normally used for emphasis.

Example 1: Да там на хер такие цены!

Translation: They got such freaking prices there!

Иди на хер - A milder version of fuck you (иди на хуй), something like "go to hell".

Example 1: Что? Да иди ты на хер!

Translation: What? Screw you!

Херово - Badly. A euphemism for хуево.

Example 1: Херово получилось.

Translation: It worked out badly.

Хрен – Euphemism for dick (хуй).

Example 1: Где этот хрен?

Translation: Where is this dick?

Нах – Euphemism for «на хуй». Normally used for emphasis.

Example 1: Я пошел в кино нах.

Translation: I'm going to freaking movies.

На хрен - Euphemism for «на хуй». Normally used for emphasis.

Example 1: Там на хрен никого нет

Translation: There's no one freaking there!

Иди на хрен - A milder version of fuck you (иди на хуй), something like "go to hell".

Example 1: Да иди ты на хрен!

Translation: Screw you!

Хреново – Badly. A euphemism for хуево.

Example 1: Денег больше нет? Хреново.

Translation: No more money? Freaking sucks.

Swearing is a part of every language and there is no reason it should be neglected, especially when one's goal is to become proficient in every aspect of Russian. At the same time, keep in mind that it's important to get a feel of these words before you use them freely as some don't sound so bad in English but can be extremely offensive in Russian. Thus, be sure to listen to how other people use them and rely on common sense. Finally, use these responsibly to make sure no one gets hurt, whether physically or emotionally.

-8-

Index of Words/Phrases

Бздеть / Набздеть – To Fart.

Бля - Slut

Блядина - Slut

Блядища - Slut

Блядовать – To whore around.

Блядский - Whoreish

Блядство - Slutiness

Блядь - Slut.

Говниться / Заговниться – To act difficult.

Говно – Shit.

Говно на палочке – Shit on a stick.

Говноед – Shiteater.

Говнюк – Shithead.

Гондон – Condom (Douchebag).

До пизды – Don't give a fuck.

До хуя – A shitload.

Доебываться / Доебаться – Fuck with.

Долбоеб – Dumbfuck.

Дрочить / Подрочить – Jerk off.

Ебало – Ugly mug.

Ебальник – Ugly mug.

Ебанат – Ugly mug.

Ебанный – Fucking.

Ебанутый – Fucked in the head.

Ебануть / Ебнуть – To hit.

Ебанушка – A fuck up.

Ебать мозги – Fuck with my head.

Ебать Му Му – Same as ебать мозги.

Жопа – An ass.

Жопа с ушами –Ass with ears. Same as previous.

Жопа с ручкой – Ass with a handle.

Жополиз – Asslicker.

Заебись – Fuck yeah.

Заебывать / Заебать – To get sick of.

Зажопивать / Зажопить – Withhold something valuable.

Иди на хуй – Fuck you (literally go on a dick).

Какого хуя? – What the fuck?

Манда – Cunt.

Мне по хуй – I don't give a fuck.

Мудак – Moron.

Мудило – Moron.

Мудозвон – Moron.

На хуй так делать? – Why the fuck do that?

Наебывать / Наебать – To swindle/cheat someone out of something.

Отъебись – Fuck off.

Педераст – Faggot.

Педрило – Faggot

Пидар – Faggot.

Пидараз – Faggot.

Пизда – Cunt.

Пизда Ивановна – Cunt.

Пизданутый – Fucked in the head.

Пиздеж – Lies

Пиздец – Fucking a

Пиздить / Напиздить – To lie

Пиздить / Спиздить – To steal

Пиздюк – A bitter fuck.

Подъебывать / Подъебать – To make fun of.

Проблядушка – Slut.

Сосать / Отсосать – To Suck.

Ссученок – Son of a bitch.

Сука – Bitch.

Сукин сын – Son of a bitch.

Трахать \ Потрахать – To fuck. A milder version of fuck, this one is much less offensive.

Уебан – Same as ебанушка.

Уебок – Same as ебанушка.

Хуеплет – Dickbender.

Хуесос – Cocksucker.

Хуй – Dick.

Хуй тебе в рот – Dick in your mouth.

Хуйня – Nonsense or sucks.

Хули – Why the fuck?

Хуяк – Simulation of a hit.

Хуярить / Захуярить – To energetically do something or to hit someone.

Хуячить / Нахуячить – Same as хуярить.

Что за на хуй? - What the fuck?

Made in the USA
Lexington, KY
19 June 2011